THESE FREAKEN PARENTS

The Relationship Between
Adult Children and their Aging Parents

By

Dominic A. D'Abate, Ph.D.

Published by : Consensus Mediation Centre
(consensusmediation@me.com)

ISBN – 978-0-9952530-1-8

Cover and Chapter Images: Reproduced with permission from a painting by artist **Barbara Sala** entitled : Parallel Worlds – The Red Car

Table of Contents

Preface

This book is written as a response to the growing request from adult children, generation X and millennials, who are often dumbfounded and overwhelmed by the conduct and actions of their aging parents. We often hear distraught adult children lament that "their freaken parents" are sometimes driving them crazy. According to them, they often act like spoiled baby boomers on a mission who don't listen while refusing to take any advice. Worse, there are many parents who threaten to cut off all contact with their adult children if they are remotely criticized or not given respect and obedience they feel they deserve. Much like their parents, the natural and most common response from adult children is, often, to react emotionally and from what they consider to be a practical and realistic perspective that is more in tune to the reality of modern life.

The laments of parents that were presented in a complimentary book (these Freaken Kids) are echoed, in their own right, by this new generation of children who consider themselves to be open-minded, liberal, self-expressive, upbeat, and passionate about having their rights and needs respected. Perhaps more than their less technological savvy parents, the 'boomerang generation' as they are otherwise known, are truly masters of information retrieval and the use of social media as enlightenment and inspiration and as a guide to their actions. What they lack in wisdom and life experience, they more than make up in the conviction that the 'good old days' are not the only point of reference in the way things should be done. The world around them is fast paced and demanding and requires that they multi-task and muster all of their energy and the few resources they possess just to stay afloat and survive. Relations with their more 'complacent' and 'out of touch' parents who rely on set way of doing things become naturally strained and conflict ridden. Patience, compromise and subtlety are not their strong suit giving rise to expectations and demands that their parents often find difficult to understand and meet. As the latter struggle to exercise their authority and parental responsibility, their adult children also become exasperated in trying to fulfill their filial responsibilities while maintaining their independence and focus on what they need to do to move on with their lives.

The quality of inter generational relations are affected by individual characteristics and, more significantly, by life transitions. For adult children, parental divorce and a decline in physical and mental health are events that greatly impact how they relate to their aging parents, as do problems in their own marriages and relationships. These and other tensional issues around financial support, moving out of the family home and the need to be more physically present will be presented in the following pages.

Alienating and Rejecting Parents – Freaked out Adult Children

What the Freaken ...

Adult children are frequently heard lamenting and expressing their deep felt resentment towards parental behaviours that have pushed them away and created bitterness and differences that have been near impossible to reconcile...

...*"My 'freaken' parents don't get it...I'm not their perfect little child that they so 'proudly raised' "*.

... *"If they could only understand, we're not living in the sixties anymore, it's the 21st century, for f... sake"*.

For some adult children, past events continue to haunt them and they cannot so easily forgive and forget...

...*"For years, my mother made my head this big, demonizing my father.. and now it's like it never happened"*.

…"I was never smart enough, ambitious enough and never thought to go anywhere… suddenly, I'm now expected to do all the right things and support them. I'm still hurt and I can't just put it behind me".

Lamented other disgruntled and exasperated off-springs…

…"They think they are always right and won't listen to anything you tell them… I'm fed up and I'm going to focus on my own family for once"

…"It's not that I don't care but what he wants to do makes no sense to me, I think he's lost his marbles"

…"And we're the selfish ones… it's unbelievable! maybe they should take another look at what they expect us to do "

What on earth is going on …

Although parents tend to see themselves more often as the victims of estrangement and rejection, many adult children have their own story to tell, one that gives another colour and dimension to the family narrative. Numerous factors can contribute to this toxic and sad state of affairs, namely, mental illness, hidden agendas and family secrets, being overly rigid and controlling and a refusal to acknowledge emotional undercurrents. At the interactional level, both parents and adult children could misinterpret what is being explicitly said (meta communication) and bring the conversation to a whole new level of conflict that can spiral out of control. Parents, with the best intentions, are often unsure how to balance wanting to be close to their children and providing them with the autonomy and distance needed for them to become self reliant. Adult children can be equally guilty of being impatient, intolerant and vindictive in response to their parents' actions.

As evidenced in the research literature, parents are sometimes subject to dysfunctional behaviours (micromanaging, emotional blackmail, creating guilt) that are indicative of serious personality disorders such as narcissistic behaviour disorder whereby parents try to validate themselves through their children, making it difficult for them to separate. Parental control is also maintained through certain histrionic emotional manipulation (victim role, guilt trips) against which most adult children fall helpless.

Some parent- adult child estrangement have a long history and is a result of long standing psycho-pathological relational behaviours usually related to the parentification of children, rejection of one particular child (sometimes based on gender or for reasons not known) and the alienation of children from parents. Parental alienation syndrome whereby a parent maliciously turns a child against a targeted parent usually during a highly contested divorce is probably the most well known and studied phenomenon that forces children to choose between a 'good parent' and a 'bad parent'. The destructive effects on children last well into adulthood when the victimized child becomes aware of the alienating actions and is faced with a myriad of feelings that include, hatred, guilt and confusion.

Irrespective of the reason for the estrangement, most adult children continue to suffer negative consequences that impact their quality of life, especially in their personal and family relationships. The way that they deal with these realities and come to term, or not, with the many emotions that are generated varies in accordance with the intensity and history of the conflict with their parents and the character make-up of the adult child involved.

The natural response...

While adult children are less distressed than their aging parents with regards to loss of contact due to estrangement, their lives are, nevertheless, negatively impacted. Not unlike their often highly emotional parents, reactions are often visceral and dictated by how intense the crisis is experienced. There are certain adult children that are so confused and uncertain of what is going on with their parents that they become indifferent and unable to take any action, choosing to remain on the sidelines...

…"They're adults and can solve their own problems…I'm not going to let that determine my life"

…"I'm still undecided as to what I should do…but I don't want my children to not have grandparents"

…"For me, there's nothing nice to say, so I'm not saying anything, period!"

Anger, mistrust and resentment linger years after….

…"Trust me, they'll do it to my son too!"

…"I'm now 37 years old and I don't know how the hell to get back the past 25 of those years I lost with my father and had to move away from my alienating mother…my focus is trying to be a good father to my own children "

And, even some hope that reconciliations is possible….

…"There's got to be a better way…I'm so stressed, I'm willing to see a counsellor as long as they also agree…and pay for it, I'm broke "

…"After everything is said, I still love my parents…if they're willing, I'll do my part"

…"My faith has been my way of coping…prayer helps and I'm slowly starting to heal…I even pray for them"

For the most part, adult children resort to strategies that include not reacting to what has been done to them and, leaving the door open for some sort of reconciliation. It should be mentioned that most adult children are connected with their parents and, as they age, will often make the extra effort to bridge the gap.

And what do the professionals advise.....

In life, there are many situations in which individuals will experience some minor or major degree of rejection that they wish to eliminate or, at least, minimize from their lives. Millennials are more apt than their aging parents to consult with professionals about their experiences and distress and explore possible ways of coping and moving forward, especially those that have had to also deal with the needs of their own immediate family. With regards to alienation and estrangement, adult children are probably more emotionally impacted and damaged than they would be as a result of other problematical issues affecting their relations with their parents. Sometimes, this negative experience starts in childhood and is prolonged over a long period of time reaching adulthood. In other instances, rifts and estrangement arise from disagreements over values and lifestyle choices that escalate into bitter and seemingly irreconcilable conflicts. At the same time, it is emphasized that the relationship between parents and adult children is very challenging and maintaining the bond is never easy, especially when transitional events occur i.e. concerns around health, re-settlement, retirement, changes in careers, start of new family, separation and divorce, etc...

What adult children should consider before doing anything

➢ Parents can reject adult children for reasons that are often not revealed or unknown making it very hard for the latter to understand what is fuelling the estrangement e.g. children born outside a marital union that was never revealed, old parental feuds that used children as pawns, secretive adoptions, etc..

➢ Misunderstandings or exaggerated reactions to what has and continues to take place between parents and adult children can easily escalate and become 'too big' to handle.

What can adult children do

➢ In those situations where adult children are treated as teenagers, a good tactic to use is to consider parents as fellow adults and to convey to them that they are no longer minor children over whom they have authority. In maintaining that position, there is a good possibility that parents will eventually begin to respond accordingly.

➢ Taking a positive and pro-active perspective, adult children can make an effort to engage their parents in an effort to respectfully discuss feelings of disappointment and resentment over particular hurtful and rejecting behaviour.

➢ Adult children should examine their own actions and attitudes (daily contact, automatically turning to a parent for help, abusing mom's willingness to baby-sit) that might, in themselves, be contributing to the strained relations with their parents. As well, adult children should not excessively rely on their parents' resources but depend more on their own ability to meet personal and family needs.

➢ It is essential for adult children to define themselves as being emotionally separate from their parents

➢ Adult children need to acknowledge the source of their hurt feelings and assume responsibility for their reactions. In many ways, adult children can have a significant influence on the quality of the relationship with their parents.

➢ If continued contact with a parent contributes to the hurt and pain already being felt, it might be a wise decision to step back and disengage from further interaction.

So, what are adult children to do...

<u>For starters</u>.....

- Become aware of your own emotional reactions and feelings of hurt and disappointment that might stem from childhood experiences

- Assess how realistic you are of the expectations and demands made of your parents

- Accept the possibility that relations with your parents will not improve and that damage control is indicated

<u>Try to avoid</u>...

... <u>expressing negative and destructive feelings</u> and views of past family relations as it will only widen the divide and push parents away

... <u>hanging on to unrealistic hopes</u> of erasing all the ills created by past interactions that continue to poison present relations

... <u>anticipating a dramatic change</u> in how parents think and what they value, old habits and convictions die hard

Finding Solutions...

✦ *In these difficult and painful situations, some young adults turn to their faith for comfort while others will use social and work related networks in search of surrogate parents and substitute families. Finding temporary or even long-term relief is an important step in moving towards a more desirable place.*

✦ *Asking yourself how would you be reacting differently with your parents if you weren't so freaked out and resentful of their rejecting and alienating behaviour, might open up other paths that you might take.*

✦ *Talk to someone (friend, professional) about the problems you are encountering with your parents. Getting a different perspective and advice can make a difference.*

Check these references...

Publications on Alienating and Rejecting Parents:

✓ Parental Alienation, Child Psychological Abuse, Parent-Child ...www.warshak.com/publications/what-is-parental-alienation.html

✓ Parental Alienation, DSM-5, and ICD-11 - Page 3 - Google Books Result
https://books.google.ca/books?isbn=0398079455

✓ Adult Children of Emotionally Immature Parents: How to ... - Amazon.ca
https://www.amazon.ca/Adult-Children-Emotionally-Immature-

✓ Adult Children of Emotionally Immature Parents: How ... - The Bookshelf
bookshelf.ca/product/view/9781626251700

On the Internet:

- Moving My Kicking-And-Screaming Elderly Parents 1,600 Miles To Be ... www.huffingtonpost.com/arlene-lassin/caring-for-elderly-

- Moving an elderly parent to live nearby — common and complicated ...www.chicagotribune.com/.../ct-talk-moving-parents-brotman-0406-   20150403-colum..

- Moving Elderly Parents Into Your Home | 10 Factors to Consider
www.caring.com › In Home Care › Receiving In-Home Care

- Assisted-Living, Aging Parents, Moving, Housing Choices, Caring for ...
www.aarp.org/relationships/family/info-09-2009/goyer_the_big_move.html

Aggressive and Toxic Parents – Indignant Adult Children

What the Freaken ...

Adult children can become quite indignant to any aggressive and demanding behaviour on the part of their parents...

... "I'm still treated as a little girl who doesn't know what she's doing!".

..."If I don't do things the way he wants", I'm being disrespectful and self centered.."

... "Talking to her makes me want to tear my hair out. I'm so angry and don't know what to do"

Another was disillusioned and perplexed

..."After so many years, it's still the same old story... it's their way or the highway"

Not surprisingly, targeted adult children are frequently heard deploring how their parents' toxic behaviour has had such a demoralizing and painful effect on them…

…"They never have anything positive to say, it's such a downer it makes me question everything I do"

… "I'm starting to question my own relationship with my husband and children".

Feelings of resentment and even anger towards their parents are typical reaction for many adult children…

…"If they had been better parents and not acted so crazy maybe things would be different now"

…"My father is so self righteous and judgemental and he doesn't even see how horrible he can be"

…"How dare them talk to my kids this way…they make *me out to be someone neglectful and who doesn't care about anything except myself"*

… "This is emotional blackmail to ask me to be a 'good daughter' and straighten out my brother… where the hell is my father in all this?"

<u>What on earth is going on ...</u>

Although parents might decry the critical and disrespectful behaviour on the part of their adult children, the latter are all too often subjected to parental behaviours that are overbearing and destructive. Most adult children are equally indignant and shocked at what they hear and are made to endure not only as they grow up but even after they have become fully independent and living on their own. Parents, in some instances, can be manipulative, self-focused, aggressive and insensitive to the needs of those closest to them resulting in behaviour that is upsetting and damaging to those in their orbit. Furthermore, there is a tendency to be very controlling and to dictate how things should be and how people should act. For these parents, nothing is ever good enough and they usually harbour unrealistic expectations of the world around them. Unlike those parents that simply suffer from some minor mental health condition, the aggressive and more toxic parent will be forceful and exert their influence and power through angry outburst, ultimatums and by using bullying tactics. Whether intentional or not, they are mean to their children and demand that they be obedient and subservient at any cost. The latter are sometimes considered competition or as an inconvenience until they suddenly are able to provide something that a parent needs or desires.

Children of aggressive and toxic parents invariably have the most difficulty in adjusting to adult life and seek the most help in their struggle to cope and survive. Being hurt by the people that you have loved and needed can be devastating and debilitating, requiring an inordinate degree of attention, support and re-assurance. The level of stress, anxiety and depression felt by these adult children far exceeds normative levels for this population. They also tend to be less productive and successful in the work force and in their social life while succumbing to frequent bouts of PSTD and in need of therapeutic assistance. The old adage that 'abusive parents breed abusive children' is also true as the latter are, sometimes, doomed to repeat behaviors that they consider unacceptable and toxic in their parents.

The natural response…

How adult children naturally respond to the antics of aggressive and toxic parents depends greatly on the extent of their childhood experience and the access these parents have to them and their own children. Typically, some will continue to endure their parents' over-bearing ways and abusive behaviour and become resigned to more of the same while others fight back and react in an equally forceful manner.

A good number of young adults respond with resignation and little hope that anything will change....

...*"My parents have always been so controlling and convinced that they have all the answers that nothing will ever make them change their ways"*

... *"It's not worth the fight and, besides, I really need their support at this point in my life".*

Others become so anxious and emotionally overwhelmed by what they have to endure that disengagement becomes the only alternative ...

...*"Every time I see my mother I have to up my medication...she won't do this to me anymore"*

..."*They can do whatever they want, but I'm deleting them from my Facebook and Skype account"*

..."*The less time I spend at home, the better. I wish I could be stronger"*

Standing up to their parents when they act abusively is not always easy for most adult children but for a determined few, it's a necessary course of action....

...*"My friends tell me I'm crazy for not telling my parents what I really think...they're right and I'm not going to let them take advantage of me anymore"*

A fortunate few have the necessary support to help them weather the storm…

…"According to my therapist, I've been victimized all these years. They need help…"

And what do the professionals advise…

As we have previously mentioned, tensions and disagreements between parents and their adult children can be considered as a normal part of the parent-child relationship, especially in some cultural communities where traditional roles are rigidly practiced. On the other hand, aggressive and abusive behaviours on the part of parents that continue to feed chaotic and unstable parent-child relations are far less justifiable and cannot be so readily dismissed. As parents need to protect themselves from their abusive children, so do children need to confront aggressive and toxic parents whose actions can be far more malicious and damaging to their well being and those of their immediate family.

What adult children should know before doing anything

➢ One of the most difficult things for adult children to deal with is when a parent acts in ways that are abusive and that undermine their well being. This is especially difficult when those parents in question take no responsibility and do not acknowledge how destructive such actions can be. Rectifying this situation and making parents accountable is not an easy task and will require an inordinate amount of patience and determination.

➤ When anyone is confronted by toxic parental behaviour, the normal reaction is to fight or take flight and deal with what the brain construes as a danger and an attack. Clear and rational thinking on the part of adult children are usually not a first course of action. Effective communication will tend to take a back seat to visceral and impulsive reactions. It is important to acknowledge that one's reactions in adulthood can be activated by past emotions and traumas experienced during a difficult upbringing that can often leave deep scars. As such, understanding the difference between past experiences and what is presently lived as an adult is helpful when considering a course of action.

Actions adult children can take

➤ Abusive behaviour can run deep and doesn't suddenly become more acceptable and positive with time or as a result of wishful thinking. Stepping away and standing firm in putting an end to what is hurtful and emotionally damaging is crucial for healing and moving forward with one's life.

18

➢ Living at home can pose particular challenges for young adults who are subjected to abusive behaviour over which they have little control. While leaving might not be possible or even desirable, it is important that some distance be created between parents and adult children who also need to spend time by themselves (as a means for self reflection and healing).

➢ In those situations where there is a steadfast refusal or inability on the part of parents to acknowledge their role and accept responsibility for their toxic behaviour, adult children have little choice but to cut off or drastically curtail contact in order to protect themselves from further harm. This could be especially difficult if these parents are older or appeal to feelings of guilt.

➢ Being a victim of abusive behaviour can be a very traumatic experience that can shape a person's view of themselves and influence future relationships with those that are loved and cherished. Adult children need to be vigilant in making sure that they are not repeating the very toxic behaviour that they decry in their parents. There is also a tendency to associate with individuals who are themselves abusive and hurtful towards others. Vigilance needs to be exercised in recognizing these tendencies and steer a different course, one that replaces undesirable behaviours and those actions that perpetuate them.

So, what is a young adult to do...

For starters.....

- *Convince yourself as a young adult that you were not responsible for the abusive behaviour endured in your childhood and that it isn't all your fault for the breakdown in your present relationship with your parents or with how they feel.*

- *Assess realistically the toxic nature of parental behaviour, namely are you being treated as a child, made to feel guilty if you disagree, are manipulated and threatened emotionally or financially, made to feel inadequate irrespective of what you do...*

- *Acknowledge that you and no one else can assume responsibility or take the necessary steps to extricate yourself from a toxic relationship that is not in your best interest.*

Avoid...

... engaging in an emotional slugfest with a toxic parent - you will probably re-live past abusive treatment and not make any headway in altering their way of thinking or acting

... taking drastic action and 'burning your bridges' as this might come to haunt you later

---

(avoid)

... <u>putting your own children in the middle of the conflict</u> and using access to them as a bargaining chip – contact with their grandparents can be beneficial to them while being toxic to you.

Finding Solutions.....

✦ Ask yourself what would change or be different if your parents would be able to relate to you in a more positive and non-abusive way. If some of these changes can actually be realized, great...but if nothing changes despite your best effort, then you need to consider other options...

✦ Putting a boundary and creating space between yourself and a toxic parent is often necessary even if sentiments of love and obligation continue to be felt. Consulting a neutral and impartial professional can be very helpful in finding the best way to disengage and move on with your life.

Check these references...

Publications on Aggressive and Toxic Pare

- ✓ Toxic Parents: Overcoming Their Hurtful Legacy and Reclaiming Your ...
  https://www.amazon.ca/Toxic-Parents-Overcoming-

- ✓ Hurtful.../dp/0553381407
  Resources and Links - If You Had Controlling Parents
  www.controllingparents.com/links.htm

- ✓ Adult Children of Emotionally Immature Parents: How ... - The Bookshelf
  bookshelf.ca/product/view/9781626251700

- ✓ J8's Book Review: Toxic Parents Overcoming Their Hurtful Legacy and ...
  https://www.pinterest.com/pin/459930180672159264/

On the Internet:

- ✓ 9 Signs You Have A Toxic Parent | Bustle
  www.bustle.com/articles/109435-9-signs-you-have-a-toxic-parent

- ✓ 8 Types of Toxic Patterns in Mother-Daughter Relationships ...
  https://www.psychologytoday.com/.../8-types-toxic-patterns-in-mother-   daughter-relati..

- ✓ Ending the Toxic Relationship and Giving Yourself Time and Space to ...
  https://theinvisiblescar.wordpress.com/.../ending-the-toxic-   relationship- and-   giving-yo.

- ✓ Transforming the Mind - Toxic Parents
  www.trans4mind.com/transformation/transform3.16.htm

When Parents Suffer from Mental Illness – Helpless and Confused Adult Children

What the Freaken ....

It is difficult enough for adult children to deal with parents when their behaviour is rejecting and toxic, but it is quite another matter when mental illness afflicts the very people who were and continue to be there to, supposedly, provide guidance and support. If parental behaviour was mysterious and challenging to deal with when growing up, you can imagine how annoying and unsettling it can be when mental health issues begin to surface as they get older. Mental illness renders people, including mom and dad, less functional and more unpredictable in everything they say and do.

Some young adults consider their parents' behaviour as disturbing and even crazy …

… *"Why is my mom acting this way? It's not normal for her to suddenly loose interest in everything…"*

... *"It was bad enough before, but now that he's getting older, he's become so much more demanding and impossible to please, it's unbearable"*

... *"I am so devastated, I just want to cry... my mother doesn't recognize me anymore, we were so close before and now we're like two strangers now"*

Many express disappointment, shame and embarrassment...

... *"My mother is not normal, she has to be always right and you can't tell her anything negative without her biting your head off – its 'freaking' embarrassing!"*

... *"What do I tell my girlfriend, I'm so upset and demoralized... I really thought that they would have gotten their act together and stopped acting so weird once my brother and I moved out and they would have had more freedom and money"*

... *"Why can't I have a normal family!"*

... *"I feel so all alone in this... but if I tell anyone, it's kind of putting your family's dirty laundry out for everyone to see "*

Leads to anxiety and worry...

... *"Is this what awaits me too? I'll kill myself if I end up like her!"*

...*"How much longer can my mother put up with his crazy behaviour, and then what's going to happen?"*

... *"After the separation, my mother's depression worsened and she literally flipped out... I hate to think what's next!"*

Anger, resentment and trepidation as to what to do and expect ...

... *"My family is as dysfunctional as they come, my mother can't deal with my father's condition anymore and my brother, well... he's nowhere to be found – this is fu.... great!"*

... *"I feel bad but hey can't expect me to give up my job and come back home to take care of things"*

... *"If he doesn't even know who he is, how is he going to survive, let alone take care of his daily needs"*

What on earth is going on...

Mental illness afflicts millions of adults and their families every year in North America. Sadly, it is estimated that nearly 5 million children in Canada and the U.S. have a parent who suffers from a mental illness such as bi-polar disorder, schizophrenia, depression, narcissistic and borderline personality disorders and severe anxiety disorder, to name a few. In many instances, these conditions go undiagnosed and, consequently, untreated while an increasing number of baby boomers suffer from Alzheimer's disease and dementia which can be easily detected but are much more difficult to treat. Furthermore, there are countless parents who suffer from PSTD (post traumatic stress disorder) that is, generally, undiagnosed and can occur without warning.

When young adults suffer from mental health issues that often interfere with studies, jobs, social and family life, they, at least, enjoy the luxury of having relatively well functioning parents who are there to pick them up and support them when they are floundering and need help. On the other hand, when it is their parents that are affected, the whole family suffers and children as well as those who are adults have to deal with an experience that is often confusing and disturbing, especially if they are obliged to remain in the family home. Several reliable studies have concluded, for example, that parental (mothers, in particular) depression and bi-polar disorders are strong predictors of adult child problems. In more general terms, research on the topic indicates that young adults who have grown up with parents suffering from mental illness are at greater risk of having emotional problems and developing similar patterns of behaviour due partly to genetic factors and learned behaviour. More disturbing and as might be expected, there is strong evidence that they have a greater tendency to not complete high school and follow through with a viable career plan, hence not having a successful 'launch' into the world. For those young adults on whom parents continue to place a huge obligation for their care (financial, social and emotional), the negative impact and burden is even more pronounced. Taking on added responsibilities in caring for an ailing parent, at any age, will invariably engender feelings of anger, uncertainty and resentment and do little to promote normal development

While many adult children of mentally ill parents generally have more problems in their ability to socialize and experience substantially more relationship and marital difficulties, there are also many others who are able to balance their filial obligations with personal needs and those related to their own children and partners.

The natural response...

Adult children, not unlike the reaction of their parents, experience much distress and confusion in having to deal with their parents' mental health problems. Some have grown up in these conditions while others have been faced with situations that they least expected and were not prepared to handle.

A common reaction, similar to that of parents, is denial and wishful thinking that, maybe there isn't a problem after all...

… *"When my mother finally decides to also retire, my father's morale is going to pick up and he's going to be less depressed about everything "*

… *"Everybody forgets things – I sometimes forget the names of many of the people I work with"*

Some adult children are uninformed as to what they are dealing with and misguided in their efforts to cope….

… *"Menopause has really changed my mother's perspective and behaviour, I can' wait until this thing is finally over."*

… *"He's always had a short fuse, you just have to know how to handle him when he's in a foul mood…which, unfortunately, is frequently"*

… *"My mother might be totally self centered but I know she really loves me…she is everything to me"*

Others create distance between themselves and their parents or simply walk away

… *"My sister has a lot more patience than me. She can take care of them given that she's right there…money is no problem and I intend to visit on Thanksgiving and Christmas."*

… *"She's has to be always right and of course that means that I'm always wrong. You know what, I don't have to put up with this s… anymore. The less I see of her the better…I just feel badly about my dad"*

And what do the professionals advise…

The professional literature and the information available on the internet on the topic of mental illness, parents and the elderly and the impact this has on children (of all ages) is prolific and quite prescriptive. While much of what has been written focuses on young children and teens, there are, increasingly, more professionals and social pundits putting their focus on the adult child–aging parent relationship. Indeed, it has become a contemporary crisis given the increase in the adult population who live longer and, consequently, are more apt to suffer from diseases such as dementia, Alzheimer and a variety of mental health disorders.

Not unlike the reaction from parents whose adult children suffer from a mental illness, the latter are often completely in the dark as to what is going on in the minds of their parents. Living with mentally ill parents is at best, unpredictable, and at worst, a constant worry that something bad will happen. Although no sure bet prescriptions are advanced, some directions is offered in terms of how adult children can begin to deal more adequately with a rather complex problem.

What adult children should know before doing anything

➢ Parents who have suffered from a mental illness for much of their lives will not suddenly recover or experience a remission. More than likely, their condition will continue to impact their lives and progressively render them less functional as they age.

➢ Having a parent with mental illness will illicit many feelings and concerns that can put into question self-identity and one's own behaviour. It is not unusual for adult children to feel guilty or responsible for the illness and wonder what they could have done to prevent it.

➢ Mental illness does not necessarily run in families or is passed on by contact or exposure to dysfunctional behaviour while growing up. Despite what they have experienced, adult children can lead perfectly normal lives and become loving and caring parents.

Being informed and having a good understanding of the situation

➢ Adult children need to be informed not only of the nature of the mental health condition that afflicts their parents but, more importantly, what is the long term prognosis and treatment.

➢ Every effort should be made to also become familiar with the social support networks available to the family and on which they can turn to when the need arises. Establishing a close contact with social workers, doctors and other resource persons is especially important.

➢ While a high percentage of ageing adults experience some form of memory loss, brain diseases like dementia and Alzheimer are much more serious conditions. The latter, for example, is irreversible and destroys brain cells, affecting thinking, memory and normal functioning. To date there is no cure or ways to prevent it from occurring.

Differentiating mental illness diagnosis

➢ As is the case for the population as a whole, mental illness is not a one size fits all. On the contrary, there is a major difference between an older person who suffers from a dementia that is caused by the normal aging process and someone who is afflicted by clinical depression, schizophrenia or anti social disorders.

➢ Aside from being better informed as to what parents are experiencing, it is important to involve a professional (social worker, psychologist, family doctor) who can assess and make a more accurate diagnosis of the problem. This can be very helpful in taking the next step, namely providing support and treatment.

When parents refuse or are not interested in getting help

➢ In general, getting parents to acknowledge that they not only have a mental health problem but that they need professional help is a frustrating and loosing proposition. These parents are often more resistant or in denial when confronted by their adult children. In fact, they can even be more stubborn in the latter situation as they feel more threatened and vulnerable as they age. Just as parents get rebuffed when they confront their adult children, so too are the latter dismissed and require the intervention of extended family members, religious leaders and trusted professionals such as a family doctor.

Intervention when dealing with less severe conditions

➢ A majority of parents will have some sort of mental health problem or illness, usually mild and short lived, during their lifetime. In most instances these conditions are not severe and can be treated by a family doctor as opposed to requiring the intervention of a psychiatrist. Getting a professional to properly assess the situation at hand can prevent either inaction or over reaction that might needlessly mobilize resources.

➤ Adult children should be made aware that when the problem is short lived and doesn't keep repeating itself (e.g. situational depression, anxiety), erratic and disturbing behaviour will eventually dissipate as the life situation of the parents improves with regards to finances, social life, use of drugs and alcohol and parenting capacity. Should a situation still become overwhelming, it is advised that adult children talk to friends, professionals or take part in organized support groups and activities.

➤ Maintaining a positive relationship with them and assuming a caretaker role can be very comforting and re-assuring to parents who otherwise would feel abandoned and not wanted.

Intervention when dealing with more serious mental illness

➤ When a parent suffers from a narcissistic personality disorder (as opposed to more healthy adult narcissism), their behaviour can be extremely confrontational and characterized by a complete disregard for the feelings or needs of everyone around them, especially towards those to whom they are bonded and love. Adult children who make an effort to interact in a rational manner or try to disregard the hurtful behaviour are generally frustrated and discouraged by the lack of progress made and the futility in trying to get the parent to understand and change. The fact of the matter is that there is little that can de done other than to create necessary boundaries and protect oneself from the negative projections.

➤ It is important to strengthen one's own positive sense of self by surrounding oneself with those that enhance rather than destroy it. When adult children are not able to do it, they risk 'serious infantile regression' whereby they continue to idolize, at all costs, the narcissistic parent as their 'saviour and protector'.

➤ In cases where dementia or Alzheimer has been diagnosed, loss of autonomy and good judgement can be expected to accompany these conditions and this may require the family members to consider restricting mobility, constant supervision and even placement. As matters can get very complicated and discouraging, it is strongly advised that adult children consider being part of a caregiver support group that brings together family members of those that are afflicted.

➤ As a last resort, adult children might need to consider the placement of a parent in a more protective environment or nursing home. This is usually a much more arduous and stressful task as most parents will tend to resist any efforts to remove them from their home. As well, even when the resistance is low, finding an available place that is compatible and affordable can be daunting and requires patients, persistence and above all professional support.

Self care

➤ Having lived in an household where one or both parents have experienced bouts with mental illness or having been suddenly confronted with such a situation in later years, adult children are often in need of counselling or coaching and should seek the services of a trained professional to help them deal with the myriad of feelings involved as well as helping them to step back and consider all of their options from a more rational perspective.

➤ Joining self-help groups set up for people like themselves who need support and information can only help and, in some more toxic and complex situations, it can become an important life line.

➤ Given the challenges and demands that face adult children, it becomes important to work together with other siblings and family members and seek the support of the community and professionals. As well, it is vitally important for significant others (partners and spouses) to be brought on board, if not in an active role, at least in one that is supportive. Family mediators can be engaged to help siblings arrive at a consensus in terms of a common plan of action.

So, what are adult children to do...

<u>For starters</u>.....

- Get to know and understand what is behind your parents' behaviour that is unusual and disturbing to you. You can talk to them about what they are feeling and how they are coping. Speaking with family doctors and getting a medical history of treatments and any medication that have been prescribed can often be revealing.

- Try and determine if this behaviour is new or has persisted over the years and, importantly, whether it is putting them and those around them at risk. Determining what is serious and what is merely 'odd' or 'dysfunctional' behaviour is a critical first step prior to any action taken on your part.

- Check out your own feelings and emotions that are being generated by your parents' behaviour. Ask yourself if your reaction and potential involvement is in response to a need that you have or whether there is a genuine concern for their well being.

<u>Try to avoid</u>...

..... engaging in a therapeutic or a 'parent' role before knowing exactly what it is that you are dealing with and assessing the effectiveness of your intervention

.... being critical or insensitive with regards to what your parents' might be going through

.... making it a mission to straighten everything out for your parents, especially on your own

Finding Solutions.....

- *Dealing with your parents' mental health condition can prove to be not only a major challenge but an emotionally draining experience for you and your immediate family. If you feel that you must intervene, prepare yourself in advance by collecting as much information as you can and mobilizing whatever support systems are available to you. Involving other family members and professionals can prove to be invaluable and necessary.*

- *Remember, if the problem is serious, solutions will not be readily at hand and you're in it for the long run. Self care is also strongly suggested.*

Check these references...

Publications on Parents and Mental Illness:

✓ Critical issues for parents with mental illness and their families J Nicholson, K Biebel, BR Hinden, AD Henry, L Stier - 2001 - escholarship.umassmed.edu

✓ Parents with severe mental illness and their children: The need for human services integration AK Blanch, J Nicholson, J Purcell - The journal of mental health ..., 1994 – Springe

✓ The differential effects of parental alcoholism and mental illness on their adult children OB Williams, PW Corrigan - Journal of clinical psychology, 1992 - Wiley Online Library

✓ Anxiety and depressive disorders in adult children caring for demented parents. JR Dura, KW Stukenberg... - Psychology and ..., 1991 - psycnet.apa.org

✓ The experiences of children living with and caring for parents with mental illness J Aldridge - Child abuse review, 2006 - Wiley Online Library

On the Internet:

- **Mental Illness in Families**
  www.aacap.org/AACAP/.../Children-Of-Parents-With-Mental-Illness-039.aspx

- **Children living with a mentally ill parent - Friends for Mental   Health**
  www.asmfmh.org/resources/publications/children-living-with-a-mentally-ill-parent/

- **Parents | Mental Health Foundation**

https://www.mentalhealth.org.uk/a-to-z/p/parents

- Visions - Parenting | Canadian Mental Health Association BC Division
    https://www.cmha.bc.ca/get-informed/personal-stories/visions-journal/parenting

- Adult Children Of Those With Mental Illness - Band Back Together
    www.bandbacktogether.com/adult-child-of-those-with-mental-illness/

Problems of Alcoholism and Substance Abuse
A nightmare for Adult Children

What the Freaken ....

Growing up in a family where parents abuse drugs and alcohol can be a harrowing experience for adult children who continue to feel the aftermath if not the continuation of a dysfunctional and destructive relationship with one or both of their parents. For many, the nightmare continues even after reaching adulthood and doesn't end after moving out of the family home. The emotional scars persist and efforts to extricate themselves from the influence of dysfunctional parents are not always successful. The old saying that you need to 'love them or leave them' is not easily applied for a myriad of reasons.

Initial surprise and even disbelief …

… *"It didn't dawn on me that my mother had a serious drinking problem until I was 25 -all along I thought she was just depressed and demoralized about her situation"*

… "What the freaken…my father is a minister and my mother has always been by his side carrying his bible!"

… "Well, I knew they drank socially but to find out they're hooked on booze and smoke pot, it blows my mind and I feel so helpless in doing something to help"

… "You know, in a crazy way, I'm relieved it's not something like dementia or Alzheimer's…still… "

Brings out shame, embarrassment, guilt and disappointment…

… "I moved back home after finding out about my father's 'disease' but it didn't take long for all of the past s… to resurface. Nothing's really changed and I don't know how much longer I can stay and help my poor mother "

… "It was really embarrassing to see her - wine stains on her clothes, always had a cigarette dangling from her mouth and couldn't say two words without slurring everything that came from her mouth"

… "My brother and I felt very isolated…friends and neighbours and even other family wouldn't come around anymore"

Leads to anxiety, worry and trepidation as to what to do and expect …

…"I felt anxious and worried all the time… my boyfriend couldn't understand and he left"

… "I now realize how much of an impact my mom's addiction has had on my life, and it's mostly bad"

What on earth is going on?

While baby boomers are often portrayed as a generation of optimism and achievement they have also had a reputation for living the so-called high life and are usually associated with an excess use of alcohol and drugs, such as cocaine and marijuana. While many have tended to be moderate in their consumption, others have tended to go overboard and become mired in addiction and dependence. Alcoholism, in particular, has plagued many families with children being the primary victims. It is estimated that there are well over 30 million adult children of alcoholics (ACOA) in both Canada and the United States, many of whom carry the trauma they experienced as children well into their adult years. Not only do they run the risk of themselves following in their parents' footsteps but are saddled with an emotional baggage they can't easily discard. They have a strong tendency to deny that anything is wrong and, by consequence, a disregard for personal needs and feelings while being overly concerned for those of others. Most children growing up in an alcoholic or drug dependent family are made to feel that they are different from everyone else and that they need to reconfigure the reality of their experience in order to create a semblance of normalcy. Having lived as victims of an abusive household, adult children are unfortunately attracted to similar people as partners, friends and colleagues.

As these baby boomers age, some effectively deal with their old habits and others are unable to shed their dependency. Among the elderly, addiction to prescription drugs as well as alcohol is, surprisingly, on the rise as many attempt to cope with early retirement, empty nest syndrome, serious illness and the death of a spouse or child. Over one quarter of all medication is prescribed to older persons who can easily become dependent on narcotic based painkillers, sleeping pills and tranquilizers. Self - medication and use of alcohol can follow a major life trauma or simply result from a lifestyle choice that doesn't make much sense to adult children. In fact, the latter are not always aware of the problems that arise and are invariably obliged to react unexpectedly.

The natural response...

When confronted with either a long-standing dependency problem or one that suddenly raises an ugly head, adult children are, generally, hard pressed to find the most appropriate way of responding. Reactions can be as much dictated by past experiences as they can by their present circumstances and personal disposition. Much like the reaction of their own parents to family crisis, adult children can be equally consumed by shame, regret of not having done more, and a heavy heart that keep them at their parent's beck and call...

... "I couldn't leave even though I was old enough...as it turned out I was their only life line "

..." This is really bad news but I live too far away to help out"

... "I'm expected to be the man of the family now and if I don't deal with this problem, we're all going to hell in a hand basket"

... "So what else is new, I'm not going to go through this hell again"

... "There is nothing my mother has not taken, a real junkie. I slowly moved away and got my life together with the help of my partner. I'm learning to make peace with how she decides to lead her life and not feel constantly stressed by what she says and does"

Some adult children look elsewhere for guidance and even deliverance...

… "First of all I was in shock and in denial, then I turned to my father for help"

… "I realized finally that you should never feel alone in these situations"

… "There's no hand book on how to deal with a parent's addiction"

… "It's taken a while but talking about it is really helpful…it's really a freaken disease and there's nothing shameful about getting help"

… "His doctor has said that a little wine every day is good for his heart and it relieves the pain… I guess if it were that bad we would be told"

And what do the professionals advise…

Young adults who have grown up with an alcoholic or a drug abusing parent face enormous hurdles in their attempt to move away from an environment dominated by dysfunctional family interactions. The process of healing and ensuring that one's own life is free of substances abuse is even more challenging when leaving the family home is not a realistic option. For those who have managed to set up their own household and family, recurring problems from either early or late onset addiction on the part of one or both parents will ultimately re-engage them in a caretaker role. This might resurrect old feelings that have laid dormant for years or reveal to adult children aspects of their parents' current lifestyle that were never contemplated.

What adult children should know before doing anything

➢ Getting a better understanding of what just happened or has been happening to your parent is important before any action to remedy the situation is attempted. Substance abuse and addiction among elder parents is, in most cases, a complex phenomenon that go beyond their outward manifestations and the perceptions of those involved.

➢ It is useful to distinguish the nature and history of the dependency. Early onset abusive use of alcohol and drugs is a much more common problem affecting nearly two thirds of older alcoholics and addicts while late onset abuse originates much later in life and can be caused by many different life crisis and traumas. The latter situations are much more easily treated although more difficult to initially detect given the 'surprise' element that confront those involved.

➢ Like children, some elderly parents will seek if not demand help while others will keep their dependency private and try to cleverly hide, albeit unsuccessfully, any evidence that might indicate that something is wrong.

➤ Long time addiction to alcohol and drugs can be considered more of a disease and subject to personal life choices that have been made over the years.

➤ All too often, there is a tendency to get into a panic mode that, invariably, creates excessive and misguided rescue missions or non-involvement. Refusal to admit that there is a problem is also quite common and should be anticipated and factored into whatever plan of intervention is being devised.

➤ Older parents who abuse the use of prescribed medication can loose track of the reason why such medications were prescribed in the first place. It is not unusual for the elderly to experience lapse of memory and good judgement as witnessed by those who suffer from dementia and Alzheimer's.

➤ Intervention on the part of professionals, other family members and an existing support network is usually warranted and necessary.

When parents refuse or are not interested in getting help

➤ It is not uncommon for older parents hooked on drugs and alcohol to be oblivious to the fact that they have a serious problem requiring some sort of intervention. In these instances, adult children need to consult a trained professional in the field and get some insight and direction as to how to proceed. This is especially critical when you have depressed individuals that become despondent and hopeless about their life situation or when there are serious co-morbidity factors. Some parents don't have a clue as to what is going on and even less power to make any meaningful changes. Other than denial, the rational for not doing anything is often based on a strong conviction that at a certain point in life it is one's prerogative and right to choose how to live and cope.

➢ If there is a persistent refusal to consider altering unhealthy choices but there is no imminent danger of serious harm, adult children are well advised to back off temporarily but to keep a watchful eye as to when it might be more opportune to intervene.

Intervention when dealing with substance abuse

➢ To be effective in dealing with this issue, adult children need to take a non-confrontational but caring and loving stance when interacting with their elderly parents. Also, managing one's expectations is critical as altering life long habits or dealing with the complexities of life in the 'golden years' can be quite daunting and frustrating.

➢ Elderly parents need to be placed, however difficult, on a 'checklist' with regards to their use of prescribed medication. It is also important to be vigilant about any change in behaviour that might indicate substance use and abuse, e.g. large number of empty bottles hidden throughout the house, unusual irritability and physical symptoms, ticketed for driving while drinking, legal and financial problems that can't be .

➢ If being close at hand is not always possible, getting a neighbour or other related family member to keep a close eye on vulnerable parent could be helpful.

Personal care

➢ The need for caregivers, both those who are directly and indirectly involved, to get support for themselves is important and indispensible. It can come from different sources and can consist of casual contacts with empathetic individuals as well as from more formal groups and professionals. Organizations like Al-Anon, Nar-Anon and Alzheimer's Association are but a few that offer support programs that are generally very helpful to those adult children whose parents are suffering addiction. Sharing with other individuals in similar situations can be very relieving and empowering.

So, what are adult children to do...

For starters...

- *For young adults to heal and survive the aftermath of having grown up with alcoholic or drug consuming parents, it is imperative that you find a way to separate your childhood experience and memories from the present in which you find yourself.*

- *Some distance needs to be created between yourself and a parent who continues to be a substance abuser*

- *If you are still living in the family home, you might want to clearly understand the nature and extent of the problem and the extent to which you can help your parents.*

-*Form a team with other family members, concerned neighbours or friends of your parents as well as professionals who can take over when you are not available.*

Try to avoid...

... _associating with individuals_ that have had similar past experiences or who have themselves been victims of a dysfunctional family setting

... _being alone with an overbearing parent_ who continues to abuse alcohol or drugs

... _thinking that you can change a parent's old habits_ or new lifestyle choices when they refuse to acknowledge that there is a problem or that there is a need for change

Finding Solutions...

✦ The problem of parental substance abuse, whether it be alcohol, drugs or prescribed medication can be a complicated matter, especially when it involves the elderly. Looking for permanent solutions might be more elusive than ever imagined. In most situations, damage control and managing the freaken 'nightmare' are probably more realistic and attainable goals that you can hopefully realize.

✦ Self care and acknowledging that you cannot do this alone will go a long way in ensuring that you do not become overwhelmed and over burdened with resolving a problem that, after all, is not yours in the making and for which your parents need, ultimately, to assume responsibility.

52

Check these references...

<u>Publications on Parent Alcohol and Substance Abuse:</u>

✓ *The differential effects of parental alcoholism and mental illness on their adult children OB Williams, PW Corrigan - Journal of clinical psychology, 1992 - Wiley Online Library*

✓ *Effects of Parental Substance Abuse on Children and Families www.aaets.org/article230.htm*

✓ *The effect of parental substance abuse on young people | JRF https://www.jrf.org.uk/.../effect-parental-substance-abuse-young-people*

✓ *Alcoholism And Its Effect On The Family | AllPsych allpsych.com › Journal*

✓ *Growing up with parental alcohol abuse: exposure to childhood abuse, neglect, and household dysfunction SR Dube, RF Anda, VJ Felitti, JB Croft, VJ Edwards... - Child abuse & ..., 2001 - Elsevier*

On the Internet:

- *Adult Children of Alcoholics Characteristics & Personality www.searidgealcoholrehab.com/article-adult-children-of-alcoholics.php*

- *Common Characteristics of Adult Children of Alcoholics - Verywell www.verywell.com › ... › Being an Adult Child of an Alcoholic*

- *Freeing the Parents of Adult Alcoholics and Addicts - GoodTherapy.org www.goodtherapy.org/.../freeing-the-parents-of-adult-alcoholics-and-ad...*

- *Influential Factors of Parental Substance and Alcohol Abuse on ...*

  pdxscholar.library.pdx.edu/cgi/viewcontent.cgi?article=11 02...mcnair

- *Common Relationship Challenges for Adult Children of Alcoholics www.rehabs.com/.../common-relationship-challenges-for-adult-children-.*

Caring for Aging parents – A Challenge for Siblings

What the Freaken …

Parents are, generally, expected to provide care for their children and do so with little reservation. After all, that is what parenthood dictates. On the other hand, when the roles are reversed and these same parents eventually need to be taken care of, adult children do not so easily assume the same responsibilities towards them. Tensions, aggravations and even resentment arise in the call of duty.

… "I was with them last Christmas and I they seemed to be doing o.k., all of a sudden they tell me they can't remain alone anymore "

… "I was devastated when my mother called from the hospital"

Brings out anger and disappointment…

...It makes me want to cry, she was so strong and in control of her life".

... "You know, he did have it coming with the crazy lifestyle he lead"

... " This is all coming at the wrong time...they could have been more prepared "

Leads to anxiety and worry...

..."My sister can't assume all the responsibility for their care, I wish I could do more"

..."If they both end up in a nursing home, I just don't know how they are going to survive"

... "I don't have any control over what is going to happen to them"

... "I should have done more to prepare them, especially my mother who is so overwhelmed"

What on earth is going on?

With regards to social ties, the parent-child relationship is definitely one of the most enduring and intense bonds that connect human beings to each other. At the same time, this connection, while usually a positive one, can create friction and feelings of ambivalence, especially as both parents and children get older. Tensions usually peak when aging parents become increasingly dependent on their adult children and the latter are obliged to provide for their needs. Caring for one's off springs comes natural for most parents but is often a struggle and confusing process when the roles are reversed. This is particularly the case in Western culture where children are launched out into the world, and are expected to be independent and to focus primarily on meeting their own needs. Baby boomers have always prided themselves in being self reliant and able to plan for their own future. Being dependent on others and told how to live their lives are not things that are easy for them to accept. Consequently, when adult children are obliged to get involved, they encounter resistance and resentment. As if it was not hard enough to back track on their own precarious life trajectory, adult children also face the daunting task of convincing their elderly parents that they now need help.

Complicating matters further is the fact that parents are living much longer and not necessarily in good physical and mental health. Adult children could, technically, be involved in caring for their parents for twenty or thirty years, a period during which they are also providing for the needs of their own immediate family and even an ailing spouse or parents-in-law that might equally require care and demand attention. If all of these stressors were not enough, you can add the inevitable conflict between siblings as to what, who and how things need to be done, and for what length of time.

The natural response...

Adult children are generally eager to be of help to their parents when they are in need of care but are often unsure of how this assistance should be provided or under what circumstances intervention would be most helpful. When the 'crunch' comes, many are unprepared or dumbfounded at what is happening. Emotions run high and uncertainty prevails. Helping aging parents can bring out the best and worst in adult children who, invariably, react differently. There are those that become quite anxious and demoralized and others that simply take charge from the very start.

Some adult children are uninformed as to what they are dealing with and misguided in their efforts to help....

...*"Why force her into a nursing home if she insists on staying in her own home... she has caring friends and lots of good neighbours"*

With or without the involvement of siblings .....

... "I'm the oldest of my brothers and sisters and the one that my parents turned to for help ever since I can remember... I guess I have no choice but to continue being there for them"

... "It upsets me to no end that my brother who lives close by can't be bothered to drop in on them and see what they need"

... "My older brother lives two thousand miles away and my sister can hardly take care of herself... I frankly don't expect either of them to provide any significant help"

Resignation of the inevitable...

... "Nobody asked for this situation, it 'freaks' me out but that's life, I guess"

... "You get old, you get sick...my mother as done pretty good given her age"

And what do the professionals advise...

While tensions between adult children and their aging parents tend to run high, research findings seem to indicate that both parties do, ultimately, find some sort of compromise and solution to the relationship problems experienced between them. Attempting to understand the other's point of view and accommodating their respective wishes and desires are usually met by success. In those situations, however, where tensions are quite elevated and have been present for long periods of time, this process can be much more difficult and consume a lot more energy, effort and time. There are many adult children who go to great lengths in trying to intervene with their parents in a sensitive and respectful manner while there are others who are much more brusque, impatient and forceful when coming to the aide of their parents. Nevertheless, there is a strong conviction among professional caregivers for the elderly that every effort should be made to not 'go it alone' as the engagement can become quite demanding, complex and long term.

What adult children should understand

➤ Parents tend to generally over-estimate their ability to provide for themselves as they grow older. The pride and conviction that they have the primary responsibility to take care of their children, and this unconditionally, often overshadows the fact that they too will need the be cared for at some point in their lives.

➤ Some parents are genuinely embarrassed in becoming dependent on others let alone having to ask for help even when they are no longer able to care for themselves. For some it is a sign of failure and weakness

➤ If there is ambivalence felt by some adult children who are thrust in a caretaking role, it probably has less to do with the moral character of the individual as with past experience in growing up with controlling or over permissive parents.

How can adult children assume a caring role

➤ In most instances, efforts to change parental attitudes will be met with resistance and lead to frustration in not being able to convince them of a logical course of action. As such, it is important to use a different strategy whereby parents can be encouraged to consider different options that are acceptable to them and do not pose a threat to those beliefs and attitude that they hold dear.

When should adult children intervene

➤ Knowing when to intervene in the care of aging parents is critical as getting involved too early or too late can make the difference between success and the frustration of a setback. As a general rule, engaging in an on going discussion about the need for eventual care before problems manifest themselves can keep the door open and facilitate matters when decisions have to actually be made, e.g. moving out of the home, etc. When parents are 'prepared' in advance, for having their children intervene, acceptance is more likely and will be met with less opposition.

Forming a team with siblings and other family members

➤ Unless there are no other siblings, adult children are well advised not to embark alone on any plan to care for their aging parents. Getting 'all loved' ones on board early and working as a team is enormously helpful, especially in the long stretch as this support can last for many years and become extremely costly. In order to get your siblings involved, it is important that they be accepted for who they are and how they think and to request a 'realisable' contribution from them as well as for them to continue to be actively involved on the 'team'.

➤ At the same time, this 'team work' can equally become a challenge in itself and create unwanted stress. It is strongly advised that siblings engage in a serious conversation whereby they contemplate, in advance, what role each will play. Always keep in mind that not everyone will be on the same page and at the same time or share the same perceptions as to what needs to be done. Patience and allowing individuals to work through their scepticism and even denial is critical in engaging them in the process.

➢ Most likely, someone will become the primary care provider and it becomes critical to negotiate how this person(s) will be supported and, even, compensated by the others for undertaking what could easily become a full time role. While everyone's contribution should be made in accordance to their personal circumstances, every effort needs to be made to ensure that no one ends up unfairly doing too much or too little.

➢ Family meetings need to be regularly held and should include siblings, other family members and close friends (professionals can be asked to participate from time to time). These meetings can be very helpful in clarifying and getting a better understanding of the problem, to consider the various possible options available and to finally set goals and distribute tasks and responsibilities in achieving them. These meetings can be more productive when there are clear agendas and someone to lead the discussion that is respected and trusted (sometimes getting a professional to assume that role is essential). In terms of content, it is best that family meetings, for the most part 1- focus on the present and the issues at hand 2- allow everyone a chance to express their opinion and suggestions 3- avoid blame and accusations dredged up by past events 4- keep everyone informed about outcomes of decisions made and actions undertaken.

➢ Decisions around finances can be the most contentious but important decisions made by the 'family'. Siblings should thoroughly discuss the issue and negotiate how the incurred costs will be actualized and shared, especially when time off has been taken from a regular employment. Compensation may also involve the primary caretaker getting a greater share of the 'inheritance'.

Self care

➢ Adult children who assume the role of care providers for their aging parents will usually be involved for a very long period of time and need to take whatever means necessary to ensure that their own personal, family and social needs and obligations are also met.

➢ It's not a good idea to pre-maturely quit a job or request for a leave of absence before finding out what is required in caring for parents. Significant loss of income and employment benefits could be disastrous in the long term and deprive adult children of the means of providing for their own financial needs.

So, what are adult children to do...

For Starters...

- Anticipate that your parents will need some type of care one day and that you will be called to play a role. Being prepared for that eventuality can make a huge difference for everyone concerned. Also, take stock of your feelings about becoming a caretaker or making decisions on behalf of your parents.

- If you don't live at home or nearby, make frequent trips to visit your parents and be vigilant for any signs of deteriorating health or general functioning.

- Address tactfully your observations with your parents and weave it in the on going discussion of how you and your siblings will be available to take care of their needs

---

Try to avoid...

... *relying on mom and dad's feedback* in terms of how they are doing – it can be deceiving as they will usually tell you 'I'm just fine dear'.

... *last minute salvaging efforts* as it is much harder going uphill and dealing with uncooperative parents in a crisis as well as panicking siblings

---

Finding Solutions.....

⊥ While the care of aging parents might come naturally to you, it can become a complicated process that force you to deal with many emotions and challenge you to develop problem solving skills that could easily undermine your resolve to stay the course. It is natural, at times, to feel overwhelmed, especially if you are alone and meet resistance in doing what is right and necessary in the care of those you love and towards whom you feel obligated.

⊥ Once the problem has been identifies, it is useful to make a list all the options available and involve your parents in creating a viable plan that will focus on how to best move forward in a manner that is both realistic and practical.

⊥ Above all, involve everyone you can, especially other siblings, in the search for solutions. Sometimes the input of professionals is indispensable and necessary. You should seldom feel alone in assuming all of the responsibility.

Check these references…

Publications on Caring for Aging Parents:

✓ *How to Care for Aging Parents by Virginia Morris and Robert Butler*

✓ *Coping with your Older Parents: A guide for Stressed-Out Children by Grace Lebow and Barbara Kane*

✓ *The 36 Hour Day: A Family Guide to Caring for People with Alzheimer Disease, Other Dementias, and Memory Loss in Later Life (4th Edition) by Nancy L. Mace and Peter V. Rabins*

✓ *Consumer Reports Complete Guide to Health Services for Seniors: What Your Family Needs to Know About Finding and Financing, Medicare, Assisted Living, Nursing Homes, Home Care, Adult Day Care by Trudy Lieberman*

✓ *The Complete Eldercare Planner, Second Edition: Where to Start, Which Questions to Ask, and How to Find Help by Joy Loverde*

On the Internet:

- *Aging.com*
- *Acapcommunity.com*
- *Khn.org*
- *Forbes.com*
- *www.oprah.com/health/caring-for-aging-parents-martha-beck-advice*

Aging Parents and Finances – Overwhelmed Adult Children

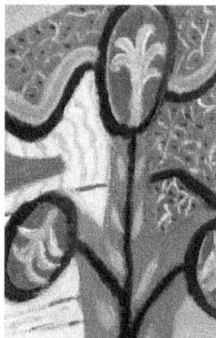

What the Freaken ..

Adult children tend to be unprepared for having to extend themselves in time and energy let alone financially for the care of aging parents....

...“It's hard enough to travel every week to be with my parents, but the extra costs involved in their basic care are killing me”

...“When my mother's money dries up, how am I going to pay her in-home help”

Some adult children are put in a double bind that clearly weigh heavily on them...

...“I'm really feeling in a bind or to put it more directly, it's a financial nightmare...my ex-wife wants her money, I have an obligation towards my kids and now this 'freaking' problem with my parents”.

Other children question the very situation in which they find themselves...

..."*Yesterday I figured the money that would be left after they passed away would lighten our debt load considerably...now it* **seems that they will have barely enough to cover the cost of care over the next couple of years".**

..."**Had I known, I wouldn't been so insistent that they travel and indulge themselves... I know, it's not a nice thing to say!"**

What on earth is going on?

The elderly today are living longer than any other generation before them and, consequently, are subject to the normal panoply of ailments and debilitating conditions accompanying old age <u>for longer periods of time</u>. As this cohort group becomes more statistically dominant, their care becomes more taxing and expensive both for the state and those individuals caring for them. It is estimated that nearly 50% of adult children are helping to support, financially, their elderly parents while an equally large number (mostly millennials) are increasingly worried that they, too, will be 'burdened' with a similar prospect once the boomer generation begin to loose their autonomy and means of support. The average assisted living arrangement can cost well over $40,000 per year and that doesn't include many added extra costs such as medical and professional care. To these costs, you can add collateral expenses related to loss of employment income and cost of travel for those children who assume a caretaking role. Even when parents remain in their own home, they, often, cannot meet most of their needs on depleting savings and what they receive from their post retirement pensions.

Given these growing realities of caring for the elderly, the old saying that 'a parent could easily care for 10 children but 10 children can barely provide for the needs of an aging parent' is, at no time, more apropos than in our present epoch.

The natural response...

As it is normal for parents to want to help their adult children, the latter are also generally inclined to reciprocate to one extent or another. Some are willing and able to provide whatever support is needed while others feel this financial responsibility as a burden that they can ill afford, especially given their own debt load or loss of income. Not unusual, the reactions of adult children vary as they tend to feel indebted to their parents and thus obliged to assist them but equally resentful that the roles have been reversed....

...“It’s not a shock to me and I’m quite sad for her.... I’ve been expecting it for a long time”

…"**Just when I'm finally seeing some light at the end of the tunnel, this has to happen"**

There are many adult children who become overwhelmed by their emotions and feelings of anger and resentment…

… **"I'm all that they have, they rely on me financially and I can't let them down"**

… *"I'd never forgive myself if anything ever happened to them…I'd rather find a safe and comfortable residence for them and forget about the extra costs"*

… *"Who knew that they would live this long and then suddenly fall ill"*

… *"My father was the stingiest man when I was growing up… now I'm expected to be generous and compassionate"*

Finally, some children take a philosophical and pragmatic view…

… *"Ultimately you can only do what you can and not what's impossible, the trick is to take a hard, long look at what is truly possible and plan to move on with that"*

And what do the professionals advise…..

Researches have found that adult children will generally provide the support their elderly parents need but doing so can be stressful and overwhelming. It takes a toll on the emotions when duty calls without much notice and with little preparation in assuming the caretaker role. Concern about how to pay for all of the unexpected needs usually raises the level of anxiety, particularly when money is tight and no provisions were made by the family for such an eventuality. Trying to piece together the financial puzzle and figuring out how to make ends meet can be a daunting task, especially when there is a shortfall and family members need to contribute. These situations are made even more challenging by the fact that aging parents are reluctant to share information let alone accepting outside help in managing their financial affairs.

What adult children should know before doing anything

➤ Given that parents often are secretive about their finances, one never really knows the extent to which they can pay for the care they need. As such, before taking any measure to help them, adult children should inquire about their parents' financial status (savings, pension income, investments and insurance coverage) and intervene accordingly.

➤ Care for the elderly can be a long term undertaking and, consequently, the costs could be staggering when calculated over many years.

➤ Parents will tend to be reluctant to ask for financial help and might minimize their needs and take shortcuts in ensuring their well being.

What adult children can do

➤ Having a serious conversation with parents, preferably before they are in need of care, is vitally important in determining to what extent they have prepared themselves (legally and financially) for the eventuality of needing assisted care. Furthermore, this information needs to be shared with any other family member involved as these costs are usually prohibitive and need to be shared by more than one stakeholder.

➤ The assistance that parents require (in home services, day center, nursing home, medical and psycho-social) should be thoroughly assessed, preferably by a competent professional (social worker or geriatric-care manager), and the costs calculated after factoring in all the available public services and coverage from existing insurance policies, Medicare/Medicaid and benefits from Veteran's Affairs.

➤ From the onset, it is important for the primary caregiver (agreed by family members) to have the possibility of accessing all of the parents' documents and financial resources including any necessary proxy to act on their behalf. To obtain this information after the fact is extremely time consuming and expensive.

➢ If parents are fortunate enough to have sufficient assets to provide for them, it is suggested that an investment manager be appointed and remain accountable to the primary caretaker on behalf of the parents and other family members. All financial transactions should be transparent and open for scrutiny as this will avoid any future questioning as to how the said assets were invested and the money spent.

So, what are adult children to do...

For Starters...

- Keep in mind that handling your aging parents' finances can be an awkward task given the role reversal and the fact that parents will not easily provide information or relinquish control of their finances.

- As such, it is wise to have parents volunteer information (on wills, bank accounts, safety deposit boxes, insurance policy) as it becomes more evident that they will need help in managing their affairs. Ask key questions while assuring them that it is necessary and you (and other family members) have their best interest at heart

- The family should assign one person who will be responsible for managing the family finances and have a professional assess the needs to be covered and the subsequent costs of care.

Avoid...

... <u>over-reacting</u> when the realities of paying for care become evident as many factors need to be taken into consideration before a final decision is taken

... <u>making arbitrary decisions</u> on your own as it will make you accountable when things go wrong and could oblige you to cover expenses that you can ill afford

---

Finding Solutions.....

- ✦ *It is hard enough for you and other family members to embark on the potentially long journey of caring for your aging parents without having to also ensure that this assistance is adequately financed, usually over long periods of time.*

- ✦ *You can more effectively meet these challenges by initially taking a full inventory of resources that are available on all levels and then creating a financial plan that will cover all other expenses over a designated period of time.*

- ✦ *Involving other family members in the decision making process can ensure that the cost of providing help to your parents will not become your sole responsibility.*

Check these references…

Publications on Aging Parents and Financial Issues:

✓ *Talking with Aging Parents about Finances - MSU Extensionmsuextension.org/publications/FamilyFinancia lManagement/MT199324HR.pdf*

✓ *Communicating with Your Parents about Finances https://books.google.ca/books?isbn=1601076525*

✓ *The Complete Guide to Managing Your Parents' Finances...www.amazon.com › Books › Business & Money › Personal Finance*

✓ *The Complete Guide to Managing Your Parents' Finances ...https://books.google.ca/books?isbn=1601383134*

On the Internet:

- *smartaboutmoney.com – an NFE site*

- *arrp.org and carp.ca - are large organizations catering to seniors*
- *www.investopedia.com/articles/retirement/11/helping-parents-manage*

- *business.financialpost.com/...finance/managing.../five-steps-you-can-take-to-help-you.*
- *https://alzheimerscareresourcecenter.com/wednesday-workshop-helping-aging-parents...*

- *http://www.wikihow.com/Help-Elderly-Parents-With-Finances*

Remaining Home or Need for Placement - Adult Children in a Frenzy

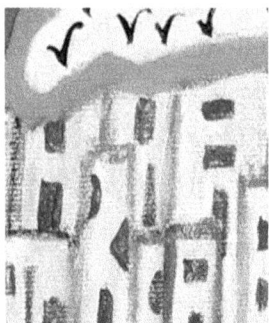

What the Freaken ...

As parents have mixed reactions when dealing with adult children who are reluctant and even refuse to leave the family home, so too, do adult children whose aging parents will invariably put them in a similar dilemma at some future time. Of all the conundrums faced by adult children none is more agonizing than that dealing with their inevitable transitioning from the family home to another more compatible setting as they become less independent...

...*"My parents have lived in the same home that my grandfather built. This is going to be one hell of a decision for them to downsize".*

... *"I finally convinced them to move to a residence for independent seniors but the place they would consider going to has a waiting list"*

...*"How crazy is this, he'll move if he can take everything he's hoarded over the years with him".*

...“My mother ended up in a wheelchair and unable to go up and down stairs...but she still insists on staying put in her cottage”

Some adult children feel they are placed between a rock and a hard place...

...“I live 400 miles away and cannot continue going back and forth to make sure that they are going to be o.k.”

...“It took me so long to finally move out, my life is going to be turned upside down with them coming to live nearby ”.

And the stress and family tensions generated by a having their parents live with them...

...“I hope my wife is going to be supportive, they really have no where else to go and, besides, there’s no money to place them elsewhere “

...“I’ll take my mother in but my father is impossible to live with...my sister has to step up here”

What on earth is going on?

Sooner or later, elderly parents loose their ability to live independently and provide for their basic needs. For some, this loss of autonomy and mobility can result from a medical condition (cancer, MS, Parkinson's, etc..) or an onset of dementia and Alzheimer's or other mental illness that considerably diminish the elderly's ability to care for themselves. The conventional life cycle following the childrearing stage is highlighted by a period whereby the 'boomer' generation generally continue to enjoy good health and functioning. As life progresses into their 60's ant 70's, maintaining accustomed living arrangements (aging in place and living in the same home and neighbourhood) often needs to be re-evaluated given the possibility of requiring institutional care. What was once adequate becomes less plausible given the changes brought about by physical incapacities, economic and social conditions.

At the same time, diminished mobility and a lower tolerance for change undermine the need to pick up roots and move forward. Lower housing costs and the unwanted stress of moving and disposing of cherished belongings are equally important factors that lead the elderly to cling to what they have. As well, alternative dwellings are usually far too expensive unless heavily subsidized. There are, certainly, some seniors that choose to downsize and move into a smaller 'condo' but these are the minority and they usually take this step when they retire and have been convinced to change their lifestyle for a 'better life'.

The natural response ...

It is a major challenge for adult children who, for whatever good reason, feel that their parents need to leave their family home and consider another more suitable living arrangement. While there are a few adult sons and daughters that choose to not get involved in such a potentially volatile process, most feel that it is their duty if not responsibility to help their parents through a most critical period in their lives. How these adult children navigate these difficult situations depends as much on their own personal life experiences as it does on the disposition and personality of the parents themselves. The following are examples of the many ways in which they perceive the problem and their, often, instinctive responses...

...*"When I visited my parents for thanksgiving, I was shocked to see an empty fridge and my father wandering about as if lost. I need to alert the neighbours and local authorities to keep a watch over them, I don't know what else I could do, moving them somewhere else would be a disaster"*

...*"My father is a stubborn man and no one is going to tell him where and how to live, especially me... maybe I can come around more often and keep in eye on them "*

...*"My sister lives nearby, she's always been caring for them ever since I can remember "*

Not unusual are the adult children who feel it is their duty to orchestrate everything for their parents whether they are in need or not...

...*"We've gone through all the stuff they've collected over the years and stored some of it. I've mad a video for them of everything else that they couldn't keep"*

...*"I hired professionals to move my parents and even decorate their new condo"*

There are adult children who feel that retirement is the appropriate time to leave the family home and scale down...

...*"I've always told my parents that the moment my father retires, they should sell everything, rent a small apartment and travel"*

...*"The kids are gone, they don't have to work anymore...so why not move on before they fall sick"*

And an element of self interest...

...*"I'm trying to convince my parents to sell me the house, I'll take care of them"*

And what do the professionals advise.....

To be sure, in the extensive literature written on caring for the elderly, the topic of moving a parent from their homes to a residence for independent seniors, a nursing home or even a live-in arrangement with a family member receives due attention and importance. In fact it is considered by many experts to be one of the most difficult decisions and action an adult child will ever take and one that will, invariably, change the course of future family relations. The what, how and when are critical considerations as adult children and their parents grapple with financial issues, family relations, and accessible community and professional resources. Certainly, many adult children have a great deal of difficulty in conveying to their aging parents the fact that they now need 'assisted living arrangements' and the direct implication of other family members and professionals. To complicate matters, many adult children have their own families and, consequently, can also feel 'sandwiched' between the responsibility of caring for their young children and their aging parents who are equally dependent on them.

What adult children should know before doing anything

➢ Seniors are generally very sensitive and reticent about having to give up their independent lifestyle let alone their homes to which they can become emotionally attached. It is common for them to become very sad and depressed in the thought of having to leave behind what has given them a sense of fulfillment and security for themselves and their family.

➤ It is a normal reaction for older parents to adamantly oppose any decision to have them move out irrespective of how logical and necessary it might be. The mere thought of being uprooted and end up in a strange environment is an anxiety producing and frightening prospect. An emphatic 'no' to any suggestion made in their best interest is a natural response to what is perceived as misguided good intentions on the part of their children.

➤ Most aging parents have spent much of their lives creating for themselves and their families a sound and secure foundation for the future. For many, it is extremely difficult to recognize that they can no longer take care of themselves.

Communicating with Aging Parents

➤ Given how difficult it is to convince elderly parents to consider alternative residential arrangement, it is strongly recommended that adult children engage them early in a dialogue about their current situation and future needs so that they are not suddenly forced to react. When there is an on-going regular conversation, parents find it easier not to feel that they have become a burden to their children and will not hide information from them.

➢ When discussing these sensitive issues with a potentially resistant parent, adult children can be most persuasive when they emphasize that they are intervening because they genuinely care and feel a strong concern for their well being, especially in the years to come.

When parents refuse or are not interested in getting help

➢ _In dealing with a resistant parent, children need to be patient and not resort to strong-arm tactics or pressure them in making a quick decision. It is far more effective to allow a resistant parent some time to ponder what actions they need to take even if it means the possibility that they will experience some further setback as a consequence.

➢ These parents have a strong need to make decisions for themselves based on their own assessment of what they determine to be their needs and the urgency to take action. Urging them to consider different options and giving them some margin of manoeuvre can encourage them to move from a rigid "no" to exploring other possibilities.

➢ When necessary, adult children need to enlist the help of other family members and health care providers who can be persuasive in getting the reluctant parent to at least agree to explore and visit other residential facilities.

➤ A power of attorney should be contemplated by the family and accorded to one individual as a pre-cautionary measure in case of severe loss of autonomy and ability to make decisions on the part of the aging parent.

Planning for Future Intervention with an Aging Parent

➤ When there is more than one sibling involved, it becomes essential that all family members find themselves on the same page in terms of drawing up a realistic plan for the move. Major conflicts can be avoided if all parties are clear about their roles and expectations and, above all, that they are giving their parents the same message. Sometimes it takes but one disgruntled sibling to undermine a well conceived plan.

➤ If adult brothers and sisters are not in agreement as to the 'what, when and how' of a potential move, the intervention of a 'family mediator' or even 'moving coach' would be useful and indispensable. In these meetings, issues that need to be addressed include: all the possible options available, type of care needed, costs involved, new roles and sharing of responsibilities and what to do with the family home that is being vacated.

➤ Good planning is even more important in those instances where adult children decide to have their aging parent(s) live with them or to maintain an existing co-habitation arrangement.

Having a Parent Move In with You

➢ Before a decision is made to have the parent move in with an adult son or daughter, consideration should be given to: the level of care needed; how much supervision and time can you realistically provide; the quality of the relationship; is your home able to accommodate your parent and their particular needs; what are the costs and who will help pay; impact on existing household; respecting whatever rules are set.

➢ Having an aging parent(s) move into a household with a caregiver's spouse and children, can be potentially problematic and can undermine the normal functioning of family life. As such, before any move is contemplated, it would be wise to consult with everyone in the immediate family to enlist their support and suggestions as to how this could be done effectively while respecting their needs and boundaries.

Dealing With Personal Needs and Emotions

➢ Aging parents are not the only ones emotionally affected by decisions to leave the family home. The feelings of guilt and constant self-questioning with regards to having made the right decision can also haunt most care providers, especially when it involves those whom we love and want to protect. Ultimately, adult children who have assumed the responsibility of caring for aging parents, need to realize and accept the fact that decisions are made in the best interest of that parent and that the move could not have been avoided. Much like dealing with difficult children, 'tough love' is sometimes the greatest love of all.

➢ Organizing respite care and enlisting the support of others can be a lifesaver in helping adult children deal with the accumulating stress in caring for their aging parents whether they are in a nursing home or living with them.

➢ In coming to terms with the barrage of emotions elicited by the difficult process of moving a parent, adult caregivers should seek the solace and support offered by family, friends, professionals and groups set up to help them.

So, what are adult children to do...

For starters...

- Anticipate your parents' eventual need to move from their home of many years to which they are usually deeply attached and reluctant to leave. Prepare yourself for strong opposition, one that will tug on your heart strings and challenge your arguments as to why they should leave in the first place.

- Initiate the possibility of a move (to a separate residence or to your home) well in advance of the eventual showdown by engaging them in a discussion of the changes taking place in their lives and the many options available to them.

- Take note of those signs that point to a diminished capacity for them to take adequate care of themselves and respectfully convey your concerns for their well-being.

- Help them create a reasonable and viable plan that they can reasonably implement in the transition to a more 'acceptable' residential arrangement.

Avoid...

... _confronting your parents in making a sudden decision_ that you might feel is logical and necessary but that they feel is drastic and not logical. Being persistent when they feel anxious and display resistance will only get them to dig in their heels.

... _presenting them with your ready made plan_ as to what they should do and where they should go.

..._over-reacting when they display distress_ and anger towards you as they do need to go through a mourning process for a deep felt loss.

Finding Solutions...

✦ Unless elderly parents are incapable of making decisions in their best interest, it is advisable that you include them in a process that will have a profound impact on the rest of their lives. They need to know that you understand how difficult it is for them to move and that their opinion matters. Expressing your concerns and commitment to what is best for them will help them, in turn, to give due consideration to your suggestions while offering their own solutions and options.

+ It is usually a good idea to include other family members in not only planning and implementing a move but in assuring that parents will continue to receive the support they need. When a transition to a nursing home or assisted care facility is being considered, it is important to also include professionals on the team.

Check these references...

<u>Publications on Moving and Aging Parents:</u>

✓ *Moving in the Right Direction: The Senior's Guide to Moving and ...*
  www.amazon.com › Books › Business & Money › Real Estate

✓ *Go! Moving Book - Downsizing Diva- Moving Seniors, Seniors Moving ...*
    movingseniors.net/go.php

✓ *Helping Seniors Move in the Right Direction: A guide for senior moving*
    seniorparentsellinghomemovingbook.com/

✓ *Chapter 8 The move into residential care - Policy Studies Institute*
  www.psi.org.uk/publications/archivepdfs/Elderly/TAB8.pdf

<u>*On the Internet:*</u>

- *Moving My Kicking-And-Screaming Elderly Parents 1,600 Miles To Be ...www.huffingtonpost.com/arlene-lassin/caring-for-elderly-*

- *Moving an elderly parent to live nearby — common and complicated   ...www.chicagotribune.com/.../ct-talk-moving-parents-brotman-0406-   20150403-colum..*

- *Moving Elderly Parents Into Your Home | 10 Factors to Consider*
www.caring.com › In Home Care › Receiving In-Home Care

92

- *Assisted-Living, Aging Parents, Moving, Housing Choices, Caring for ...* www.aarp.org/relationships/family/info-09-2009/goyer_the_big_move.html

- *Moving house gets harder the older you are, but a new guide to ... ageactionalliance.org/moving-house-gets-harder-the-older-you-are- but- a-new-guide-t...*

Parental Separation / Divorce and Lifestyle Changes – Confused and Embarrassed Adult Children

What the Freaken ....

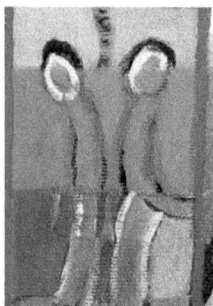

For many reason, parents are supposed to provide children with an example of stability, the highest standard of moral conduct and a sober style of living that can only be held as an example of how life should be lived. So, it is no surprise that adult children become shocked and incredulous when their parents deviate from their beaten path of a stable marriage. To be expected, their reactions vary depending on the personalities involved and the emotions and stress generated.

... "My parents have been married for over 40 years and suddenly they can't stand each other

...I don't get it!"

... " What a lousy time to decide you need a change in your life... and for what?"

Adult children are often embarrassed and disappointed when their parents decide to end their relationship or change their lifestyle...

94

... "This is really embarrassing to have to explain to my own kids and the friends that I grew up with that my mother had to ask my father to leave the house and then went to see a lawyer"

... "If they were so unhappy, why did they wait so long to separate"

... "My very conservative, church going father is now smoking up and riding around on a bike... go figure"

Still others can't believe the lack of maturity in their parents' decisions to separate...

..."They're older adults, after all...why get so excited about a little infidelity"

... "For God's sake, she's 40 years younger – where's his good sense"

Not uncommon, is the anxiety and worry...

... "My mother is left all alone.. she's sad, depressed and who knows what she's going to do"

... "It's really weird to now have to spend the holidays in two different homes"

What on earth is going on?

The number of 'gray' divorces or as some have labelled them, 'silver splitters', has skyrocketed in the past few years. Researchers have found that the number has doubled since 1990 and that one in four divorces were attributed to this population. Even among octogenarians who have spent over 50 years together in a supposedly happy union, the number of separations and divorces are inordinately high. Interestingly, this phenomenon cuts across socio-economic status, religious affiliation and even cultural background. In fact, it's not even a strictly North American occurrence as it cuts across many other countries. The reasons given for ending a marriage are many but those considered to be triggers have to do with the 'empty nest syndrome', finding a 'younger partner', the extra time couples spend together as a result of 'early retirement' and the fact that most baby boomers live longer and anticipate many years still ahead of them.

Irrespective of the root cause, the impact is huge and profoundly significant on adult children and how they perceive and integrate these new and shocking realities. They usually take it for granted that their parents' marriage is rock solid and then suddenly they are forced to deal with the fall out and demands made on them to help straighten things out.

The natural response…..

So, what do you ask, is the big deal! Well, apparently, the impact that these break-ups have on family life and on adult children, in particular, is far greater than one would imagine. One would think that adult children would be less traumatized by these events because of their age. However, when they are faced with the fall-out and demands made on them, both emotional and social, adult children react quite viscerally and are generally upset, bewildered and resentful. For most, it represents a loss and is more that they can handle. Consequently, various lenses are used to view and rationalize what has and is happening.

A common belief is that parents are being foolish and impulsive in their actions…

…"They've gone crazy and over-reacted, as usual… maybe now they can take a more sober look at want they want from each other"

…"I know my father, it's a tempest in a tea pot…he'll go back home when he's good and ready"

Some adult children are devastated but feel the pressure to help out….

... "I feel so uncomfortable but my mother is so heartbroken and sad"

... "I don't want to be his confident anymore...I've arranged for someone to talk to the both of them"

Many others convince themselves that their parents will be able to straighten out their marital problems...

... "When Diane and I separated, they were the first to suggest we go for counselling...I can't believe they won't take their own advice"

..."They're both very intelligent people who need to assess their situation in a more rational manner"

And there are those who become resigned to the inevitable...

... "No surprise...they've been unhappy and fighting since I can remember. It's better this way"

..."Not a great situation but at least they won't kill each other"

And what do the professionals advise.....

In most instances, adult children can be overwhelmed in having to deal such an unexpected decision on the part of their parents. It can easily topple many previously held beliefs and force them to re-define for themselves the meaning of family. It can easily undermine the level of security, self-confidence and reliance on values and a way of life that were once considered by them to have been stable and inviolable. Adult children equally underestimate the need to step back and take another sober look to what degree things have changed. To be sure, adult children also underestimate their need to consider how their reactions complicate matters and contribute to an already stressful situation.

There is certainly no lack of opinion or advice on the part of those who consider themselves experts in these matters as to what adult children should or should not do. The following provides a synopsis of what professionals feel are important considerations and steps that adult children need to take in dealing with their parents' decision to separate or divorce:

What adult children need to consider

➢ Unlike younger children experiencing their parents' divorce, adult children are seldom spared 'those uncomfortable situations' whereby they are provided with the often sordid details leading to the decision to separate and the parents' 'adventures' that follow. Parents' caught in an emotional frenzy forget that even adult children need to be shielded from 'too much information' about highly personal matters that do not concern them.

➢ Although of advanced age and level of maturity, older parents can easily revert back to behaviour that is more normally associated with adolescence. Expect and be prepared to hear and witness such regressive attitudes as a matter of course and that, hopefully, will subside over time. Step back and try to get a sober perspective on what is transpiring and the urgency or importance of getting involved.

➢ If there is any up side to the havoc created by the separation or divorce of parents, adult children can take note and, perhaps, improve their own chances of creating a more viable and healthy relationship by the choices they make and by paying attention to what didn't work in their parents' marriage.

Adult children caught in a conflict of loyalty

➢ Often adult children are drawn into efforts by their parents to validate their actions and sympathize with their plight and suffering. Whenever this occurs, adult children can respectfully but firmly insist that it is more appropriate to share their feelings with the other parent rather than with them. While this is not what they want to hear, eventually they will get the message.

➢ In some exceptional situations, one parent will be forceful and even aggressive towards the other. Adult children, while otherwise advised to generally stay out of the conflict, sometimes need to become involved if abusive or violent behavior is suspected or rears its ugly head. In these unfortunate situations, direct intervention is not only warranted but strongly advised. When this occurs, adult children might be the only ones who can intervene and have no choice but to protect a vulnerable parent who is being victimized.

Assuming responsibility for 'needy' parents

➢ As is often the case, one or both parents will present such a desperate need to be heard and supported that adult children will have little choice but to get involved, especially in the early stages of separation when emotions run high and rational behavior is at an ebb. A parent being told that they are no longer wanted or loved can become extremely depressed or react with anger and vengeance. Adult children will, inevitably, be drawn into the conflict and, invariably, be put in a conflict of loyalty with each parent pulling them in their respective corners. It is in these precarious instances when adult children need to exercise fortitude and a strong determination to remain neutral while ensuring that neither parent feels abandoned or rejected. It is important for them to clearly explain to their parents that it is too painful for them take sides but that they, nevertheless, love them both and will always be there for support.

➤ Playing therapist or mediator in their parents' divorce is rarely productive and can exacerbate already frail relations that adult children have with their parents. If necessary, involve third parties that are trained to play those roles.

Questions over finances and family assets

➤ While divorce may put an end to a couple relationship, it is often the beginning of on going conflict over money and family assets as potential new benefactors are introduced to the 'family'. Whether new spouses lay claim to the family patrimony or parents commit to them financially, adult children tend to be put in a difficult position trying to ensure a fair and equitable partition. It is generally recommended that a 'family meeting' take place between the parent in question, the siblings and, if possible, the other parent, in an effort to discuss any dispute that needs to be resolved. Hiring a family mediator, specializing in such matters, is also recommended when little progress is being made towards a satisfactory agreement.

New significant others joining the 'family'

➤ A parent with a new partner might be so absorbed in the new relationship that they forget that they have children that depend on them or are attached to them emotionally. Adult children can easily feel rejection and a sense of abandonment that can even extent to the grandchildren. Normally, such behaviour is short lived, nevertheless, parents need to be made aware of how their actions impact their children and that they need to become more inclusive and not abandon the 'family of origin'. Most parents will welcome such input from their adult children, especially if it is done in a manner that avoid blame and guilt.

Getting help and support

➢ Unless an only child, adult children would do well to discuss their parents' separation and divorce with their siblings and try to come up with a common plan of action that can be implemented together. Parents will also find it helpful if they are not given different messages and caught in a conflict of loyalty involving their children, the new spouse and the other parent.

➢ As these predicaments can elicit strong emotions and open up old wounds, adult children who become overwhelmed and unable to cope are advised to get support from a professional counsellor or self help groups set up to assist family members who struggle to adapt

➢ Adult children should remember that, despite research findings to the contrary, they are not doomed to repeat, in their own romantic relationships and marriages, the actions or errors of their parents. They can steer in a different directions and, effectively, avoid some of the pitfalls experienced by their 'unprepared' parents. It is helpful to always remain mindful of ones' own relationship needs and seek couple counselling or coaching when necessary.

So, what are adult children to do...

For starters...

- When your emotionally frantic parent (s) announce to you that they will be divorcing, take a deep breadth, step back and tell yourself that this is probably not a new development but has been brewing for some time.

- As in any crisis, those experiencing distress tend to be emotionally overwhelmed and unable to evaluate what is happening in a rational manner. Your parents, like any person going through a similar trauma, are, first and foremost, in need of understanding, love and some compassion.

- Listen to their story and the reasoning behind their decision as they often just need a sympathetic ear and are not necessarily eliciting a reaction or advice.

Try to avoid...

...reacting emotionally or disregarding what they are announcing as they are probably in a state of crisis and don't need more distress

...being critical or judgemental with regards to the decisions they are making

...asking too many questions or making them feel foolish or guilty – this is not what they want to hear and they usually don't have any 'good' answers to offer you anyways

---

Finding Solutions...

↓ *Your parents are mature adults (if you think otherwise, indulge them in that belief) who decided to separate or divorce for reasons that may even have escaped them. It is, nevertheless, their decision to make and their responsibility, primarily, to deal with whatever collateral damage is created.*

↓ *As an adult son or daughter, you will, invariably, be drawn into this drama and obliged to react in various ways that will significantly elevate your stress level. Getting them to come up with their own solutions as opposed to imposing your own is probably the best way for you to help and, in the process, spare yourself and your immediate family pain and aggravation.*

↓ *Above all, don't travel this road alone but include siblings and professional help.*

Check these references...

Publications on Divorce and Parents:

✓ **The Way They Were: Dealing with Your Parents'
   Divorce ... - Amazon.ca**https://www.amazon.ca/Way-
   They-Were-Lifetime-Marriage/dp/1400082102

✓ **A Grief Out of Season: When Your Parents Divorce in
   Your Adult Years ...**https://www.amazon.ca/Grief-Out-
   Season-Parents-Divorce/dp/0316363510

✓ **10 Helpful Books about Divorce for Parents and
   Children - MWI** web.mwi.org/divorce.../10-Helpful-
   Books-about-Divorce-for-Parents-and-Children

On the Internet:

- **The effect of divorce upon grown-up offspring | Life and
  style | The ...**
  www.theguardian.com › Lifestyle › Family-

- **How to Move on From Your Parents' 'Grey Divorce' -
  Huffington Post**
  www.huffingtonpost.com/.../how-to-move-on-from-
  your-grey-divorce_

- **Tips for Adult Children Who Grieve their Parents'
  Divorce - HG.org**
  https://www.hg.org/article.asp?id=32532

- **Why It's So Hard for Adults When Their Parents
  Divorce**
  www.youbeauty.com/life/why-grey-divorce-sucks-for-

<u>adult-children/</u>

- The effect of divorce upon grown-up offspring | Life
  and style | The ...
  www.theguardian.com › Lifestyle › Family

- How to Be Supportive of Divorcing Parents As an Adult
  www.wikihow.com › Home › Categories › Family Life ›
  Divorce

- When the "Kids" Aren't Kids – Divorceinfo.com
  divorceinfo.com/adultchildren.htm

Needs of Adult Children

Much like their parents, adult children have expressed their own frustrations in having to deal with their parents' actions and dispositions, hence the lament of 'these freaken parents'. For them, family life and relations are seen from a different perspective and with generational lenses that reflect their own values, expectations and priorities. It is, therefore, not unusual or surprising that the sense of obligation and commitment to the parent–child relationship and, by extension, to the family, is not nearly as strong or enduring as that of their parents.

While it is much easier for them to respond critically to what they consider to be unacceptable behavior and demands made on them, adult children too struggle in ensuring that their needs are met and their rights respected. In many ways, these needs do not differ very much from those of their parents and can be briefly outlined as follows:

✓ Many adult children have often been victimized growing up in the care of dysfunctional parents and continue to suffer mistreatment and abuse well into adulthood. It is high time that you free yourself from their dominance and put an end to toxic parental behavior.

✓ Adult children are generally torn between attending to their parents' needs and providing for the their own pressing needs of those of their new family. In this scenario there should be no room for feeling guilty for not doing enough.

✓ There are probably not enough hours in the day to allow you to fulfill all that is demanded of you, leaving you little time for yourself without having to worry about everyone else. You also deserve a little respite and peace.

✓ It is not unreasonable for you to expect that your parents act less onerously and stubbornly when they are obliged to make changes in their lives.

✓ Parents often place high expectations on their children, especially as they grow old and become less independent. Being human and limited in energy, time and resources, you will probably never fully rise to the occasion, and that's o.k. You can only do the best you can.

✓ The demands made on you can become overwhelming and tax your energy, available time, and financial resources. These precious assets might run short far too easily, so manage them well.

✓ Adult children are just that, adults, who are responsible for their own lives and can demand this need to be acknowledged and respected by their parents.